D0776523

INTEREST AND EFFORT IN EDUCATION

BY

JOHN DEWEY

SOUTHERN ILLINOIS UNIVERSITY PRESS

CARBONDALE AND EDWARDSVILLE

FEFFER & SIMONS, INC.

LONDON AND AMSTERDAM

Library of Congress Cataloging in Publication Data
Dewey, John, 1859–1952.
    Interest and effort in education.
    (Arcturus books AB129)
    Reprint of the ed. published by Houghton Mifflin,
Boston, in series: Riverside educational monographs; with
new pref.
    1. Interest (Psychology)   2. Educational psychology.
I. Title.   II. Series: Riverside educational monographs.
LB1065.D38   1975   370.15   74–18471
    ISBN 0–8093–0716–2

ARCT
URUS
BOOKS ®

CONTENTS

PREFACE

BY JAMES E. WHEELER

In the preface to the 1913 Riverside Press edition of *Interest and Effort in Education,* the distinguished university president, the late Henry Suzzallo, said that "active acceptance by teachers [of the substance of Dewey's argument presented in the book] would bring about a complete transformation of classroom methods." Intrigued, apparently, by his own appreciation of Dewey's analysis of the meaning of interest and effort, he went on to say that if parents and teachers could know only "one treatise in educational procedure, it undoubtedly should be this book." A rereading of the book sixty years or so later leaves one with the same impression, but one's enthusiasm is tempered by the fact that so little change in "educational procedures" and "classroom methods" has occurred in the intervening years. Our immediate judgment

PREFACE

is disappointed: there has been no "active acceptance by teachers" of Dewey's analysis of the meaning of the terms "interest" and "effort"; there has been no correlative redirection to attitudes and methods essential to good teaching.

In any event, the state of discussion of the themes presented by Dewey in *Interest and Effort* among practitioners and interested parents is not significantly different from that of the pre–World War I period. When some of the fundamental premises of the book, those taken from an earlier work, "Interest in Relation to Training of the Will," were first presented at Jacksonville, Florida, in 1896, conference records show the same evidence of what appears to be the willful refusal to consider seriously the major arguments. It is not that the critics (or some of them) of that time or ours have mastered the argument and sought to refute it; it is not that reasons have been given to support a belief that the conclusions are not true or . are confused in meaning. Rather, it seems that there has been a simple unwillingness to accept as serious or even tolerable any discussion of the issues insofar as a discussion may add anything to the meanings and interpretations of "interest" and "effort" hallowed by tradition.

This is not, of course, to say that there has been no serious discussion of the critical themes of this book: rather, it is to say that serious discussion has been infrequent, and that it has not greatly influenced the commonsense view of the matter today or the common practices of the school. There is an unwillingness to accept any refinement of the key terms. There is a tendency to cling to the dualism of the traditional argument.

It must be that it is a very difficult thing for people to explore ideas in terms other than the familiar and customary ones. It must be equally difficult to explore problems in a strict contextual sense; that is to say, to hold meaning strictly to account in context and to refuse to allow familiar but inappropriate meanings to affect the terms employed. Part of the problem of reading Dewey is owing, one supposes, to his insistence upon the controlling influence of context and upon his refusal to use traditional terms in contextually irrelevant ways. *Interest and Effort* is a fine illustration of Dewey's refusal to accept the customary meanings and of his insistence on meanings developed within the educational "situation" in which they are employed.

Dewey noticed quite early in his intellectual development that some philosophical and theoretical puzzles were owing to inadequate analyses of the meanings of the terms in which the puzzles are couched. Not infrequently he found a puzzle arises because an inappropriate context is set; thus, inappropriate rules for the use of terms are developed and employed. Let us consider, for example, the "commonsense" table and the "scientific" table. Which is the "real" table: the scientific table that apparently is mostly "empty space," or the commonsense table that is manifestly "solid"? Well, one is as "real" as the other: the one in the context of some scientific theory of atomic and molecular structure; the other in the context of the commonsense use of a table as an object upon which other objects rest. The "puzzle" is contrived.

It should be noticed that no compromise between two points of view and no eclectic stance is involved in an analysis of this kind. A genuinely new *perspective* is provided, and an extremely illumi-

PREFACE

nating one. It is just this new perspective that Dewey invites us to adopt in analyzing the meanings of "interest" and "effort." The error that has given rise to puzzles in this respect is common to both sides of the controversy. The error, as Dewey points out, is the assumption of the "externality of the object, idea, or end to be mastered to the self." Should one see the object, idea, or end as internal to the "growing self," so that the agent can be himself, then the puzzle of the relation of interest and effort in educational theory and practice disappears.

"Effort" arises as an attempt to realize the ends identified with the growing self; "interest" is unified activity. The entire essay is to be regarded as an exegesis upon this point.

If one sees interest as unified activity and effort as that which brings together diverse and apparently irrelevant elements in the unified activity (and excludes truly irrelevant ones), then a discussion of how to—or should one—make a subject interesting takes on a new significance. Thus, the traditional and unacceptable notion of making a subject interesting by use of external attractions is transformed and the reconstructed notion now be-

PREFACE

comes highly pertinent to classroom methods and educational procedures.

Since the potential of Dewey's analysis for school practice is so great, at least in Suzzallo's view and mine, and the effect so small, one may ask whether reasonable people should not revise their initial judgments. One may ask whether a determination to issue a new edition of this book is not merely whimsical and likely to be of little effect. The answers to these questions are not easy ones. But if one believes that well-conceived educational theory is greatly needed just now; that it is time for a discourse that raises fundamental issues; and that what passes for theory in current literature is, as theory, hopelessly inadequate; then the introduction into the present discussion of one of the great classics of the theory of education is quite appropriate, indeed is desperately needed.

One can say these things, but perhaps they are less than convincing. What may be more to the point is to note that education does have a fine and rich intellectual and theoretical tradition which serves as a critical base to illuminate practice. Even if we think theory has no effect right now, there is a way of looking at theoretical arguments so that we can be interested in theory only as theory. Theory, as a theory, has its own claim (an aesthetic and intrinsic one) upon us, appeals to us in reflective moments, and serves as a clue as to where we are and what we are doing. The initial themes and arguments of *Interest and Effort* serve as well in this respect. One simply cannot read the book, if he is at all inclined toward reflection, without considering anew his own perspective on education, on the processes of enculturation and socialization, on the lives of children. A sense of a purer understanding and an intensified insight is the almost inevitable consequence of a rereading of this book—that is, again, if one is at all intellectually inclined. Dewey is one of those people whose own thoughts add a measure of depth and clarity to our own. His perspectives, somehow, suggest to us a way of unifying what we know and feel, thus providing a firm base for action. This is so even when the exigencies of a given time and place frustrate appropriate action. Are there better reasons for reading anything?

Why is it that Dewey's thoughts, read reflectively, leave us with a sense of a greater integrity in our own? He is, notoriously, not easy to read. Someone in comparing Dewey to Peirce and James said something like this: Not so clever in matters of science and logic as Peirce, not so brilliant in rhetoric as James, Dewey nonetheless is the toughest and most rugged thinker of them all. Perhaps his appeal lies just here: his is a tough, rugged character, and his is a tough, rugged system of thought, deeply rooted in experience, rich in conception, dogged in keeping steadily on the point. Dewey's entire intellectual development is a fine example of a mind that develops under the equal burdens of firsthand experience and the struggle for conceptual clarity. It can be said of Dewey that he had the nerve to follow where the argument led; it must be said, in addition, that he had the courage not to be fooled no matter *where* the argument led. If he was not in a position immediately to find a flaw in a train of thought, his own good sense kept him at it until he did find the flaw or until the reconstruction of thought relieved the sense of flaw.

In his earliest thought one can see a promise of things to come. In his latest thought appear echoes of insights achieved early; they may be transformed by the manifold relations and the complex conceptual system in which they are found finally, but the traces are there. Not all intellectual careers have this characteristic. Russell, for example, like the moon and as brilliantly, went through phases. If the development of Dewey's thought may be likened to the continuous process by which the pony matures to the horse, Russell's may be likened to the way in which a tadpole becomes a frog. There is not much promise in the tadpole of the frog or much trace in the frog of the tadpole. The brilliance of Russell's rhetoric may be owing to his remarkable ability and willingness to follow the flow of argument wherever it leads. He had the courage to follow and to accept the outcome. Dewey, on the other hand, could never forget his tough good sense; and until inquiry could transform it, he held steadily to it. There is a genuine appeal here: one may not be in a position to point to the flaw in the logic; one nevertheless refuses to be fooled.

Seen thus, Dewey's prose, contrary to the claim that it is labored, repetitive, difficult, takes on a quality which reveals it to be effectively related to his purposes. His prose becomes not labored but natural in relation to the outcome; not repetitive but sensitive to the varying perspectives; perhaps difficult but true to the subject matter. It is the hope of one who writes this way about Dewey's prose that he may persuade those who read Dewey to do so without prejudice and to stand ready to find in what they read the qualities and integrity that are there. Perhaps, then, he may persuade himself that the expectations of Professor Suzzallo and the hopes of the present writer for an "active acceptance" of Dewey's views by teachers actually will be fulfilled.

INTEREST AND EFFORT
IN EDUCATION

INTEREST AND EFFORT IN EDUCATION

I

UNIFIED VERSUS DIVIDED ACTIVITY

In the educational lawsuit of interest *versus* effort, let us consider the respective briefs of plaintiff and defendant. In behalf of interest it is claimed that it is the sole guarantee of attention; if we can secure interest in a given set of facts or ideas, we may be perfectly sure that the pupil will direct his energies toward mastering them; if we can secure interest in a certain moral train or line of conduct, we are equally safe in assuming that the child's activities are responding in that direction; if we have not secured interest, we have no safeguard as to what will be done in any given case. As a matter of fact, the doctrine of discipline has not succeeded. It is absurd to suppose that a child gets more intellectual or mental discipline when he goes at a matter unwillingly than when he goes at it out of the fullness of his heart. The theory of effort simply says that unwilling attention (doing something disagreeable because it is disagreeable) should take precedence over spontaneous attention.

Practically the appeal to sheer effort amounts to nothing. When a child feels that his work is a task, it is only under compulsion that he gives himself to it. At every let-up of external pressure his attention, released from constraint, flies to what interests him. The child brought up on the basis of "effort" acquires marvelous skill in appearing to be occupied with an uninteresting subject, while the real heart of his energies is otherwise engaged. Indeed, the theory contradicts itself. It is psychologically impossible to call forth any activity without some interest. The theory of effort simply substitutes one interest for another. It substitutes the impure interest of fear of the teacher or hope of future reward for pure interest in the material presented. The type of character induced is that illustrated by Emerson at the beginning of his essay on *Compensation*, where he holds up the current doctrine of compensation as implying that, if you only sacrifice yourself enough now, you will be permitted to indulge yourself a great deal more in the future; or, if you are only good now (goodness consisting in attention to what is uninteresting) you will have, at some future time, a great many more pleasing interests — that is, may then be bad.

While the theory of effort is always holding up to us a strong, vigorous character as the outcome of its method of education, practically we do not get such a character. We get either the narrow, bigoted man who is obstinate and irresponsible save in the line of his own preconceived aims and beliefs; or else a character dull, mechanical, unalert, because the vital juice of spontaneous interest has been squeezed out.

We may now hear the defendant's case. Life, says the other theory, is full of things not interesting that have to be faced. Demands are continually made, situations have to be dealt with, which present no features of interest. Unless one has had previous training in devoting himself to uninteresting work, unless habits have been formed of attending to matters simply because they must be attended to irrespective of the personal satisfaction they afford, character will break down or avoid the issue when confronted with the serious matters of life. Life is not a merely pleasant affair, or a continual satisfaction of personal interests. There must be such continual exercise of effort in the performance of tasks as to form the habit of dealing with the real labors of life. Anything else eats out the fiber of character and leaves a wishy-washy, colorless being; a state of moral dependence, with continual demand for amusement and distraction.

Apart from the question of the future, continually to appeal even in childhood days to the principle of interest is eternally to excite, that is, distract the child. Continuity of activity is destroyed. Everything is made play, amusement. This means over-stimulation; it means dissipation of energy. Will is never called into action. The reliance is upon external attractions and amusements. Everything is sugar-coated for the child, and he soon learns to turn from everything that is not artificially surrounded with diverting circumstances. The spoiled child who does only what he likes is an inevitable outcome.

The theory is intellectually as well as morally harmful. Attention is never directed to the essential and important facts, but simply to the attractive wrappings with which the facts are surrounded. If a fact is repulsive or uninteresting, it has to be faced in its own naked character sooner or later. Putting a fringe of fictitious interest around it does not bring the child any nearer to it than he was at the outset. The fact that two and two make four is a naked fact which has to be mastered in and of itself. The child gets no greater hold upon the fact by having attached to it amusing stories of birds or dandelions than if the simple naked fact were presented to him. It is self-deception to suppose that the child is being interested in the numerical relation. His attention is going out to and taking in only the amusing images associated with this relation. The theory thus defeats its own end. It would be more straightforward to recognize at the outset that certain facts having little or no interest, must be learned and that the only way to deal with them is through effort, the power of putting forth activity independently of any external inducement. In this way only is the discipline, the habit of responding to serious matters, formed which is necessary for the life that lies ahead of the child.

I have attempted to set forth the respective claims of each side of the discussion. A little reflection will convince us that the strong point in each argument lies not so much in what it says in its own behalf as in its attacks on the weak places of the opposite theory. Each theory is strong in its negations rather than in its position. It is not unusual, though somewhat surprising, that there is generally a common principle unconsciously assumed at the basis of two theories which to all outward appearances are the extreme opposites of each other. Such a common principle is found on the theories of effort and interest in the one-sided forms in which they have already been stated.

The common assumption is that of the externality of the object, idea, or end to be mastered to the self. Because the object or end is assumed to be outside self it has to be *made* interesting; to be surrounded with artificial stimuli and with fictitious inducements to attention. Or, because the object lies outside the sphere of self, the sheer power of "will," the putting forth of effort without interest, has to be appealed to. The genuine principle of interest is the principle of the recognized identity of the fact to be learned or the action proposed with the growing self; that it lies in the direction of the agent's own growth, and is, therefore, imperiously demanded, if the agent is to be himself. Let this condition of identification once be secured, and we have neither to appeal to sheer strength of will, nor to occupy ourselves with making things interesting.

The theory of effort means a virtual division of attention and the corresponding disintegration of character, intellectually and morally. The great fallacy of the so-called effort theory is that it identifies the exercise and training of mind with certain external activities and certain external results. It is supposed that, because a child is occupied at some outward task and because he succeeds in exhibiting the required product, that he is really putting forth will, and that definite intellectual and moral habits are in process of formation. But, as a matter of fact, the exercise of will is not found in the external assumption of any posture; the formation of moral habit cannot be identified with ability to show up results at the demand of another. The exercise of will is manifest in the direction of attention, and depends upon the spirit, the motive, the disposition in which work is carried on.

A child may externally be entirely occupied with mastering the multiplication table, and be able to reproduce that table when asked to do so by his teacher. The teacher may congratulate himself that the child has been exercising his will power so as to form right habits. Not so, unless right habit be identified with this ability to show certain results when required. The question of educative training has not been touched until we know what the child has been internally occupied with, what the predominating direction of his attention, his feelings, his disposition has been while he has been engaged upon this task.

8

UNIFIED VERSUS DIVIDED ACTIVITY

If the task appeals to him merely as a task, it is as certain psychologically, as is the law of action and reaction physically, that the child is simply engaged in acquiring the habit of divided attention ; that he is getting the ability to direct eye and ear, lips and mouth, to what is present before him so as to impress those things upon his memory, while at the same time he is setting his thoughts free to work upon matters of real interest to him.

No account of the educative training actually secured is adequate unless it recognizes the division of attention into which the child is being educated, and faces the question of what the worth of such a division may be. External mechanical attention to a task as a task is inevitably accompanied by random mind-wandering along the lines of the pleasurable.

The spontaneous power of the child, his demand for realization of his own impulses, cannot be suppressed. If the external conditions are such that the child cannot put his activity into the work to be done, he learns, in a most miraculous way, the exact amount of attention that has to be given to this external material to satisfy the requirements of the teacher, while saving up the rest of his powers for following out lines of sug-gestion that appeal to him. I do not say that there is absolutely no moral training involved in forming these habits of external attention, but I say that there is also a question of moral import as to the formation of habits of intellectual dissi-pation.

While we are congratulating ourselves upon the well-disciplined habits which the pupil is ac-quiring (judged by his ability to reproduce a les-son when called upon) we forget to commiserate ourselves because his deeper nature has secured no discipline at all, but has been left to follow its own caprices and the disordered suggestions of the moment. I do not see how anyone can deny that the training of habits of imagination and lines of emotional indulgence is at least equally important with the development of certain out-ward habits of action. For myself, when it comes to the moral question, not merely to that of prac-tical convenience, I think it is infinitely more important. Nor do I see how anyone at all familiar with the great mass of existing school work can deny that the greater part of the pupils are gradually forming habits of divided attention. If the teacher is skillful and wide-awake, if she is what is termed a good disciplinarian, the child will indeed learn to keep his senses intent in certain ways, but he will also learn to direct his thoughts, which should be concentrated upon subject matter if the latter is to be significant, in quite other directions. It would not be wholly palatable if we had to face the actual condition of the majority of pupils that leave our schools. We should find this division of attention and the resulting disintegration so great that we might cease teaching in sheer disgust. None the less, it is well for us to recognize that this state of things exists, and that it is the inevitable outcome of those conditions which exact the simulation of attention without securing its essence.

The principle of " making " objects and ideas interesting implies the same divorce between object and self. When things have to be *made* interesting, it is because interest itself is wanting. Moreover, the phrase is a misnomer. The thing, the object, is no more interesting than it was before. The appeal is simply made to the child's love of something else. He is excited in a given direction, with the hope that somehow or other during this excitation he will assimilate something otherwise repulsive. There are two types of pleasure. One is the accompaniment of activity. It is found wherever there is successful achievement, mastery, getting on. It is the personal phase of an outgoing energy. This sort of pleasure is always absorbed in the activity itself. It has no separate existence. This is the type of pleasure found in legitimate interest. Its source lies in meeting the needs of the organism. The other sort of pleasure arises from contact. It marks receptivity. Its stimuli are external. It exists by itself as a pleasure, not as the pleasure of activity. Being merely excited by some external stimulus, it is not a quality of any act in which an external object is constructively dealt with.

When objects are made interesting, this latter type of pleasure comes into play. Advantage is taken of the fact that a certain amount of excitation of any organ is pleasurable. The pleasure arising is employed to cover the gap between self and some fact not in itself having interest.

The result is division of energies. In the case of disagreeable effort the division is simultaneous. In this case, it is successive. Instead of having a mechanical, external activity and a random internal activity at the same time, there is oscillation of excitement and apathy. The child alternates between periods of overstimulation and of inertness, as is seen in some so-called kindergartens. Moreover, this excitation of any particular organ, as eye or ear, by itself, creates a further demand for more stimulation of the same sort. It is as possible to create an appetite on the part of the eye or the ear for pleasurable stimulation as it is on the part of taste. Some children are as dependent upon the recurrent presence of bright colors or agreeable sounds as the drunkard is upon his dram. It is this which accounts for the distraction and dissipation of energy characteristic of such children, for their dependence upon external suggestion, and their lack of resources when left to themselves.

INTEREST AND EFFORT

The discussion up to this point may be summarized as follows: Genuine interest is the accompaniment of the identification, through action, of the self with some object or idea, because of the necessity of that object or idea for the maintenance of a self-initiated activity. Effort, in the sense in which it may be opposed to interest, implies a separation between the self and the fact to be mastered or task to be performed, and sets up an habitual division of activities. Externally, we have mechanical habits with no mental end or value. Internally, we have random energy or mind-wandering, a sequence of ideas with no end at all, because they are not brought to a focus in action. Interest, in the sense in which it is opposed to effort, means simply an excitation of the sense organ to give pleasure, resulting in strain on one side and listlessness on the other.

But when we recognize there are certain powers within the child urgent for development, needing to be acted out in order to secure their own efficiency and discipline, we have a firm basis upon which to build. Effort arises normally in the attempt to give full operation, and thus growth and completion, to these powers. Adequately to act upon these impulses involves seriousness, absorption, definiteness of purpose; it results in formation of steadiness and persistent habit in the service of worthy ends. But this effort never degenerates into drudgery, or mere strain of dead lift, because interest abides — *the self is concerned throughout. Our first conclusion is that interest means a unified activity.*

II

INTEREST AS DIRECT AND INDIRECT

WE now come to our second main topic, the psychology of interest. I begin with a brief descriptive account. Interest is first active, projective, or propulsive. We *take* interest. To be interested in any matter is to be actively concerned with it. Mere feeling regarding a subject may be static or inert, but interest is dynamic. Second, it is objective. We say a man has many interests to care for or look after. We talk about the range of a man's interests, his business interests, local interests, etc. We identify interests with concerns or affairs. Interest does not end simply in itself, as bare feelings may, but is embodied in an object of regard. Third, interest is personal; it signifies a direct concern; a recognition of something at stake, something whose outcome is important for the individual. It has its emotional as well as its active and objective sides. Patent law or electric inventions

16

or politics may be a man's chief interest; but this implies that his personal well-being and satisfaction is somehow bound up with the prosperity of these affairs.

These are the various meanings in which common sense employs the term interest. The root idea of the term seems to be that of being engaged, engrossed, or entirely taken up with some activity because of its recognized worth. The etymology of the term *inter-esse*, "to be between," points in the same direction. Interest marks the annihilation of the distance between the person and the materials and results of his action; it is the sign of their organic union.[1]

1. The active or propulsive phase of interest

[1] It is true that the term interest is also used in a definitely disparaging sense. We speak of interest as opposed to principle, of self-interest as a motive to action which regards only one's personal advantage; but these are neither the only nor the controlling senses in which the term is used. It may fairly be questioned whether this is anything but a narrowing or degrading of the legitimate sense of the term. However that may be, it appears certain that controversy regarding the use of interest arises because one party is using the term in the larger, objective sense of recognized value or engrossing activity, while the other is using it as equivalent to a selfish motive.

takes us back to the consideration of impulse and the spontaneous urgencies or tendencies of activity. There is no such thing as absolutely diffuse impartial impulse. Impulse is always differentiated along some more or less specific channel. Impulse has its own special lines of discharge. The old puzzle about the ass between two bundles of hay is only too familiar, but the recognition of its fundamental fallacy is not so common. If the self were purely passive or purely indifferent, waiting upon stimulation from without, then the self illustrated in this supposed example would remain forever helpless, starving to death, because of its equipoise between two sources of food. The error lies in assuming any such passive condition. One is always already doing something, intent on something urgent. And this ongoing activity always gives a bent in one direction rather than another. The ass, in other words, is always already moving toward one bundle rather than the other. No amount of physical cross-eyedness could induce such mental cross-eyedness that the animal would be in a condition of equal stimulation from both sides. Wherever there is life there is activity, an activity having some tendency or direction of its own.

In this primitive condition of spontaneous, impulsive activity we have the basis of natural interest. Interest is no more passively waiting around to be excited from the outside than is impulse. In the selective or preferential quality of impulse we have the fact that at any given time, if we are awake at all, we are always interested in one direction rather than another. The condition either of total lack of interest, or of impartially distributed interest, is as mythical as the story of the ass in scholastic ethics.

2. The objective side of interest. Every interest, as already said, attaches itself to an object. The artist is interested in his brushes, in his colors, in his technique. The business man is interested in the play of supply and demand, in the movement of markets, etc. Take whatever instance of interest we choose, and we shall find that, if we cut out an object about which interest clusters, interest itself disappears relapsing into empty feeling.

Error begins in supposing the object already

there, and then calling the activity into being. Canvas, brushes, and paints interest the artist, for example, because they help him discover and promote his existing artistic capacity. There is nothing in a wheel and a piece of string to arouse a child's activity save as they appeal to some instinct or impulse already active, and supply it with means of execution. The number twelve is uninteresting when it is a bare, external fact; it has interest (just as has the top or wheelbarrow or toy locomotive) when it presents itself as an instrument of carrying into effect some dawning energy or desire — making a box, measuring one's height, etc. And in its difference of degree exactly the same principle holds of the most technical items of scientific or historic knowledge — whatever furthers action, helps mental movement, is of interest.

3. We now come to the emotional phase. Value is not only objective but also subjective. There is not only the thing which is projected as valuable or worth while, but there is also appreciation of its worth.

The gist of the psychology of interest may,

accordingly, be stated as follows : An interest is primarily a form of self-expressive activity — that is, of growth that comes through acting upon nascent tendencies. If we examine this activity on the side of what is done, we get its objective features, the ideas, objects, etc., to which the interest is attached, about which it clusters. If we take into account that it is *self*-development, that self finds itself in this content, we get its emotional or appreciative side. Any account of genuine interest must, therefore, grasp it as out-going activity holding within its grasp an object of direct value.

There are cases where action is direct and immediate. It puts itself forth with no thought of anything beyond. It satisfies in and of itself. The end *is* the present activity, and so there is no gap in the mind between means and end. All play is of this immediate character. Purely æsthetic appreciation approximates this type. The existing experience holds us for its own sake, and we do not demand that it takes us into something beyond itself. With the child and his ball, the amateur and the hearing of a symphony, the present object engrosses. Its value is there, and is there in what is directly present.

On the other hand, we have cases of indirect, transferred, or technically speaking, mediated interest. Things indifferent or even repulsive in themselves often become of interest because of assuming relationships and connections of which we were previously unaware. Many a student, of so-called practical make-up, has found mathematical theory, once repellent, lit up by great attractiveness after studying some form of engineering in which this theory was a necessary tool. The musical score and the technique of fingering, in which the child finds no interest when it is presented as an end in itself, when it is isolated, becomes fascinating when the child realizes its place and bearings in helping him give better and fuller utterance to his love of song. Whether it appeals or fails to appeal is a question of relationship. While the little child takes only a near view of things, as he grows in experience he becomes capable of extending his range, and seeing an act, or a thing, or a fact not by itself, but as part of a larger whole. If this whole belongs to him, if it is a mode of his own movement, then the thing or act which it includes gains interest too.

Here, and here only, have we the reality of the idea of "making things interesting." I know of no more demoralizing doctrine — when taken literally — than the assertion of some of the opponents of interest that *after* subject-matter has been selected, *then* the teacher should make it interesting. This combines in itself two thorough-going errors. On one side, it makes the selection of subject-matter a matter quite independent of the question of interest — that is to say of the child's native urgencies and needs ; and, further, it reduces method in instruction to more or less external and artificial devices for dressing up the unrelated materials, so that they will get some hold upon attention. In reality, the principle of "making things interesting" means that subjects be selected in relation to the child's present experience, powers, and needs; and that (in case he does not perceive or appreciate this relevancy) the new material be presented in such a way as to enable the child to appreciate its bearings, its relationships, its value in connection with what already has significance for him. It is *this bringing to consciousness of the bearings of the new material* which constitutes the reality, so often perverted both by friend and foe, in "making things interesting."

In other words, the problem is one of *intrinsic* connection as a motive for attention. The teacher who tells the child he will be kept after school if he does n't recite his geography lesson better[1] is appealing to the psychology of mediate interest. The old English method of rapping knuckles for false Latin quantities is one way of arousing interest in the intricacies of Latin. To offer a child a bribe, or a promise of teacher's affection, or promotion to the next grade, or ability to make money, or to take a position in society, are other modes. They are cases of transferred in-

---

[1] I have heard it argued in all seriousness that a child kept after school to study has often acquired an interest in arithmetic or grammar which he did n't have before, as if this proved the efficacy of "discipline" *versus* interest. Of course, the reality is that the greater leisure, the opportunity for individual explanation afforded, served to bring the material into its proper relations in the child's mind — he "got a hold" of it.

terest. But the criterion for judging them lies just here: How far is one interest externally attached to another, or substituted for another? How far does the new appeal, the new motive, serve to interpret, to bring out, to *relate* the material otherwise without interest? It is a question, again, of *inter-esse*. The problem may be stated as one of the relations of means and end. Anything indifferent or repellent becomes of interest when seen as a means to an end already commanding attention; or seen as an end that will allow means already under control to secure further movement and outlet. But, in normal growth the interest in means is not externally tied on to the interest in an end; it suffuses, saturates, and thus transforms it. It interprets or revalues it — gives it a new significance. The man who has a wife and family has thereby a new motive for his daily work — he sees a new meaning in it, and takes into it a steadiness and enthusiasm previously lacking. But when he does his day's work as a thing intrinsically disagreeable, as drudgery, simply for the sake of the final wage-reward, the case is quite different. Means and end remain remote; they do not permeate one another. The person is no more really interested in his work than he was before; in itself, it is a hardship to be escaped from. Hence he cannot give full attention to it; he cannot put himself unreservedly into it. But to the other man every stroke of work may literally mean his wife and baby. Externally, physically, they are remote; mentally, with respect to his plan of living, they are one; they have the same value. In drudgery on the contrary means and end remain as separate in consciousness as they are in space and time. What is true of this is true of every attempt in teaching to "create interest" by appeal to external motives.

At the opposite scale, take a case of artistic construction. The sculptor has his end, his ideal, in view. To realize that end he must go through a series of intervening steps which are not, on their face, equivalent to the end. He must model and mold and chisel; perform a series of particular acts, no one of which exhibits or *is* the beautiful form he has in mind, and every one of which represents the putting forth of personal energy.

INTEREST AS DIRECT AND INDIRECT

But because these are necessary means in the achieving of his activity, the meaning of the finished form is transferred over into these special acts. Each molding of the clay, each stroke of the chisel, is for him at the time the whole end in process of realization. Whatever interest or value attaches to the end attaches to each of these steps. He is as much absorbed in one as in the other. Any failure in this complete identification means an inartistic product, means that he is not really interested in his ideal. Upon the other hand, his interest is in the end regarded as an end *of* the particular processes which are its means. Interest attaches to it because of its place in the active process of what it is but the culmination. He may also regret the approach of the day that will put an end to such an interesting piece of work. At all events, it is not the mere external *product* that holds him.

We have spoken freely of means and ends because these terms are in common use. We must, however, analyze them somewhat to make sure they are not misunderstood. *The terms " means "*

*and " end" apply primarily to the position occu-
pied by acts as stages of a single developing activity,* and only secondarily to things or objects.
The end really means the final stage of an activity,
its last or terminal period; the means are the
earlier phases, those gone through before the activity reaches its termination. This is plainly seen
in, say, the leisurely eating of a meal, as distinct
from rushing through it to have it over as soon as
possible; in the playing of the game of ball, in
listening to a musical theme. In each case there
is a definite outcome; after the meal is eaten, there
is a certain amount of food in the system; when
the nine innings of the game of baseball are ended,
one side or the other has won. Henceforth —
afterwards — it is possible to separate the external result from the process, from the continuous
activity which led up to it. *Afterwards* we
tend to separate the result from the process; to
regard the result of the process as the end and
the whole process as simply a means to the external result. But in civilized society, eating is
not merely a means to getting so much food.
power into the system; it is a social process, a

time of family and friendly reunion ; moreover, each course of the meal has its own enjoyment just as a matter of *partaking* of food, that is, of an active continuing process. Division into means and end hardly has any meaning. Each stage of the entire process has its own adequate significance or interest ; the earlier quite as much as the latter. Even here, however, there is a tendency' to keep the best till the last—the dessert comes at the end. That is, there is a tendency to make the *last* stage a *fulfilling* or consummating stage.

In the hearing of the musical theme, the earlier stages are far from being mere means to the later ; they give the mind a certain set and dispose it to anticipate later developments. So the end, the conclusion, is not a mere last thing in time ; it *completes* what has gone before ; it settles, so to speak, the character of the theme as a whole. In the ball game, the interest may intensify with every passing stage of the game ; the last inning *finally* settles who wins and who loses, a matter which up to that time has been in suspense or doubt. In the game, the last stage is not only the last in time, but also settles the character of the entire game, and so gives meaning to all that has preceded. Nevertheless the earlier parts of the game are true parts of the game; they are not mere means for reaching a last inning.

In these illustrations we have seen how the last stage may be the fulfilling, the completing, or consummating of all that has gone before, and may thus decide the nature of the activity as a whole. In no case, however, is the end equivalent simply to an external result. The mere fact that one side won — the external result or object — is of no significance apart from the game whose conclusion it marks. Just so, we may say that the value of x in an algebraic equation is 5. But to say in general that x equals 5 is nonsense. This result is significant only as the outcome of a particular process of solving a particular equation. If, however, the mathematical inquiry is carried on to deal with other connected equations, it is possible to separate the result, 5, from what led up to it, and in further calculating to use 5 independently of the equation whose solution it was. This fact introduces a further complication.

Many, most, of our activities, are interconnected. We not only have the process of eating the meal, but we have the further use of the food eaten — its assimilation and transformation into energy for new operations. The musical theme heard may represent a step in a more continuous process of musical education. The outcome of the game may be a factor in determining the relative standing of two clubs in a series of contests. An inventor of a new telephonic device is preoccupied with the different steps of the process; but when the invention is completed, it becomes a factor in a different set of activities. When the artist has finished his picture, his question may be how to sell that picture so as to get a living for his family. This fact of the employment of the result of one course of action as a readymade factor in some other course leads us to think of means and ends as fixed things external to an activity, and to think of the whole activity as a mere means to an external product. The ball game is thus thought of as a mere means to winning, and that winning in turn as a mere means to winning a series. Winning the series may in turn be regarded as a mere means of getting a sum of money or a certain amount of glory, and so on indefinitely. Unless discussion is to get confused, we must therefore carefully distinguish between two senses of the term end. While the activity is in progress, "end" simply means an object as standing for the culminating stage of the whole process; it represents the need of looking ahead and considering what we are now doing so that it will lead as simply and effectively as possible into what is to be done later. *After* the activity has come to its conclusion, "end" means the product accomplished as a fixed thing. The same considerations apply to the term "means." During the activity it signifies simply the materials or ways of acting involved in the successive stages of the growth of an activity up to its fulfillment. After the activity is accomplished, its product as detached from the action that led up to it may be used as a means for achieving something else.

INTEREST AS DIRECT AND INDIRECT

This distinction is not a merely theoretical one, but one that affects the whole scope and significance of interest in teaching. The purely adventitious interests we have discussed — making a thing interesting by the sugar-coating method — assumes a certain ready subject-matter — a subject-matter existing wholly independently of the pupil's own activity. It then asks how this alien subject-matter may be introduced into the pupil's mind; how his attention may be drawn away from the things with which it is naturally concerned and drawn to this indifferent, readymade external material. Some interest, some bond of connection, must be found. Prevalent practices and the training and disposition of the teacher will decide whether the methods of "hard" or of "soft" pedagogy shall be resorted to; whether we shall have a "soup-kitchen" type of teaching or a "penitentiary" type. Shall the indifferent thing (indifferent because lying outside of the individual's scheme of activities) be made interesting — by clothing it with adventitious traits that are agreeable; or by methods of threats — by making

33

attention to it less disagreeable than the consequences of non-attention so that study is a choice of the lesser of two evils?

Both of these methods, however, represent failure to ask the right question and to seek for the right method of solution. What course of activity exists already (by native endowment or by past achievement) operative in the pupil's experience *with respect to which the thing to be learned, the mode of skill to be acquired, is either a means or an end?* What line of action is there, that is to say, which can be carried forward to its appropriate termination better by noting and using the subject-matter? Or what line of action is there, which can be directed so that when carried to its completion it will naturally terminate in the things to be learned? The mistake, once more, consists in overlooking the activities in which the child is already engaged, or in assuming that they are so trivial or so irrelevant that they have no significance for education. When they are duly taken into account the new subject-matter is interesting on its own account in the degree in which it enters into their operation.

34

INTEREST AS DIRECT AND INDIRECT

The mistake lies in treating these existing activities as if they had reached their limit of growth ; as if they were satisfactory in their present shape and simply something to be excited; or else just unsatisfactory and something to be repressed.

The distinction between means and ends external to a process of action and those intrinsic to it enables us to understand the difference between pleasures and happiness. In the degree in which anybody externally happens to fall upon anything and to be excited agreeably by it, pleasure results. The question of pleasure is a question of the immediate or momentary reaction. Happiness differs in quality from both a pleasure and a series of pleasures. Children are almost always happy, joyous — and so are grown people — when engaged consecutively in any unconstrained mode of activity — when they are occupied, busy. The emotional accompaniment of the progressive growth of a course of action, a continual movement of expansion and of achievement, is happiness;—mental content or peace, which when emphatic, is called joy, delight. Persons, children or adults, are interested in what they can do successfully, in what they approach with confidence and engage in with a sense of accomplishment. Such happiness or interest is not self-conscious or selfish ; it is a sign of developing power and of absorption in what is being done. Only when an activity is monotonous does happiness cease to attend its performance, and monotony means that growth, development, have ceased ; nothing new is entering in to carry an activity forward. On the other hand, lack of normal occupations brings uneasiness, irritability, and demand for any kind of stimulation which will arouse activity — a state that easily passes into a longing for excitement, for its own sake. Healthy children in a healthy family or social environment do not ask, "What pleasure can I have now?" but "What can I *do* now?" The demand is for a growing activity, an occupation, an interest. Given that, happiness will take care of itself.

There is no rigid, insurmountable line between direct and indirect interest. As an activity grows more complex, it involves more factors. A child who is simply building with blocks has an activity of very short time span; his end is *just* ahead of what he is doing at the moment — namely, to keep on building so that his pile grows higher — does not tumble down. It makes no difference to him just what he makes, as long as it stands up. When the pile tumbles, he is content to start over again. But when he aims at something more complicated, the erection of a certain kind of structure with his blocks, the increased complexity of the end gives the cycle of his actions a longer time span; arrival at its end is postponed. He must do more things before he reaches his result, and accordingly he must carry that result in mind for a longer time as a control of his actions from moment to moment. Gradually this situation passes over into one where an immediate activity would make no appeal at all were it not for some more remote end which is valuable and for the sake of which intervening means, not of themselves of concern, are important. With trained adults an end in the distant future, a result to be reached only after a term of years, may stimulate and regulate a long series of difficult intervening steps which, in isolation

37

from the thought of the end, would be matters of total indifference, or even repellent. From this side, then, the development of indirect interests is simply a sign of the growth or expansion of simple activities into more complex ones, requiring longer and longer periods of time for their execution, and consequently involving postponement of achieving the end which gives decisive meaning and full worth to the intervening steps.

Not only, however, does the direct interest in an object pass thus gradually and naturally into indirect interest as the scope of action is prolonged, but the reverse process takes place. Indirect values become direct. Everybody has heard of the man who at first is interested in an acquisition of money because of what he can do with it and who finally becomes so absorbed in the mere possessing of gold that he gloats over it. This clearly expresses an undesirable instance of the change of means into end. But normal and desirable changes of the same kind are frequent. Pupils who are first interested in, say, number relations, because of what they can do with these relations in making something else (at first interested, that is, in a branch of arithmetic simply as a means or tool), may become fascinated by what they can do with number on its own account.[1]

Boys who are at first interested in skill in playing marbles or ball simply because it is a factor in a game which interests them, become interested in practicing the acts of shooting at a mark, of throwing, catching, etc., and so arduously devote themselves to the perfecting of skill. The technical exercises that give skill in the game become themselves a sort of a game. Girls who are interested in making clothes for a doll, simply for the sake of the interest in playing with dolls, may develop an interest in making clothes till the doll itself becomes simply a sort of an excuse, or at least just a stimulus, for making clothes.

If the reader will reflect upon his own course of life over a certain period of time, he will find that the sort of thing which is somewhat trivially illustrated in these examples is of constant oc-

[1] In our usual terminology interest in " concrete " number passes into an interest in " abstract " number.

39

currence. He will find that wherever his activities have grown in extent and range of meaning (instead of becoming petrified and fossilized), one or other (or both) of two things has been going on. On the one hand, narrower and simpler types of interest (requiring a shorter time for their realization) have been expanding to cover a longer time. With this change they have grown richer and fuller. They have grown to include many things previously indifferent or even repulsive as the value of the end now takes up into itself the value of whatever is involved in the process of achieving it. On the other hand, many things, that were first of significance only because they were needed as parts of an activity of interest only as a whole, have become valued on their own account. Sometimes it will even be found that they have displaced entirely the type of activity in connection with which they originally grew up. This is just what happens when children outgrow interests that have previously held them; as when boys feel it is now beneath them to play marbles and girls find themselves no longer interested in their dolls.

INTEREST AS DIRECT AND INDIRECT

Looked at superficially, the original interest seems simply to have been crowded out or left behind. Examined more carefully, it will be found that activities and objects at first esteemed simply because of their place within the original activity have grown to be of more account than that for the sake of which they were at first entertained. In many cases, unless the simpler and seemingly more trivial interest had had sway at the proper time, the later more important and specialized activity would not have arisen. And this same process can be verified in adult development as well, *as long as development goes on.* When it ceases, arrest of growth sets in.

We are now in a position to restate, in a more significant way, the true and the false ways of understanding the function of interest in education, and to formulate a criterion for judging whether the principle of interest is being rightly or wrongly employed. *Interest is normal and reliance upon it educationally legitimate in the degree in which the activity in question involves growth or development. Interest is illegitimately used in the degree in which it is either a symp-*

41

tom or a cause of arrested development in an activity.

These formulæ are of course abstract and far from self-explanatory. But in the light of our prior discussion their significance should be obvious. When interest is objected to as merely amusement or fooling or a temporary excitation (or when in educational practice it does mean simply such things), it will be found that the interest in question is something which attaches merely to a momentary activity *apart from its place in an enduring activity* — an activity that develops through a period of time. When this happens, the object that arouses (what is called) interest is esteemed just on the basis of the momentary reaction it calls out, the immediate pleasure it excites. "Interest" so created is abnormal, for it is a sign of the dissipation of energy; it is a symptom that life is being cut up into a series of disconnected reactions, each one of which is esteemed by itself apart from what it does in carrying forward (or developing) a consecutive activity. As we have already seen, it is one thing to make, say, number interesting by merely attaching to it other things that happen to call out a pleasurable reaction ; it is a radically different sort of thing to make it interesting by introducing it so that it functions as a genuine means of carrying on a more inclusive activity. In the latter case, interest does not mean the excitation due to the association of some other thing irrelevant to number ; it means that number is of interest because it has a function in the furtherance of a continuous or enduring line of activity.

Our conclusion, then, is not simply that some interests are good while others are bad ; but that true interests are signs that some material, object, mode of skill (or whatever) is appreciated on the basis of what it actually does in carrying to fulfillment some mode of action with which a person has identified himself. Genuine interest, in short, simply means that a person has identified himself with, or has found himself in, a certain course of action. Consequently he is identified with whatever objects and forms of skill are involved in the successful prosecution of that course. This course of action may cover greater or shorter time according to circumstances, particularly according to the experience and maturity of the person concerned. It is absurd to expect a young child to be engaged in an activity as complex as that of an older child, or the older child as in that of an adult. But some expansion, enduring through some length of time, is entailed. Even a baby interested in hitting a saucer with a spoon is not concerned with a purely momentary reaction and excitation. The hitting is connected with the sound to follow, and has interest on that account; and the resulting sound has interest not in its isolation, but as a consequence of the striking. An activity of such a short span forms a direct interest, and spontaneous play activities in general are of this sort. For (to repeat what has already been said) in such cases it is not necessary to bear the later and fulfilling activities in mind in order to keep the earlier activities agoing and to direct their manner of performance and their order or sequence. But the more elaborate the action, the longer the time required by the activity; the longer the time, the more the consummating or fulfilling stage is postponed; and the longer the postponement, the greater the opportunity for the interest in the end to come into conflict with interest in intervening steps.

The next step in the discussion consists in seeing that effort comes into play in the degree in which achievement of an activity is postponed or remote; and that the significance of situations demanding effort is their connection with thought.

III

EFFORT, THINKING, AND MOTIVATION

WHAT is it that we really prize under the name of effort? What is it that we are really trying to secure when we regard increase in ability to put forth effort as an aim of education? Taken practically, there is no great difficulty in answering. What we are after is *persistency, consecutiveness,* of activity: endurance against obstacles and through hindrances. Effort regarded as mere increase of strain in the expenditure of energy is not in itself a thing we esteem. Barely in itself it is a thing we would avoid. A child is lifting a weight that is too heavy for him. It takes an increasing amount of effort, involving increase of strain which is increasingly painful, to lift it higher and higher. The wise parent tries to protect the child from mere strain; from the danger of excessive fatigue, of damaging the structures of the body, of getting bruises. Effort as mere strained activity is thus not what we prize. On the other hand,

EFFORT, THINKING, AND MOTIVATION

a judicious parent will not like to see a child too easily discouraged by meeting obstacles. If the child is physically healthy, surrender of a course of action, or diversion of energy to some easier line of action, is a bad symptom if it shows itself at the first sign of resistance. The demand for effort is a demand for *continuity* in the face of difficulties.

This account of the matter is so obvious as to lie upon the surface. When we examine into it further, however, we find it only repeats what we have already learned in connection with interest as an accompaniment of an *expanding* activity. Effort, like interest, is significant only in connection with a *course* of action, an action that takes time for its completion since it develops through a succession of stages. Apart from an end to be reached, effort would never be anything more than a momentary strain or a succession of such strains. It would be a thing to be avoided, not so much for its disagreeableness as because nothing comes of it save exposure to dangers of exhaustion and accident. But where the action is a developing or growing one, effort, willingness to put forth energy at any point of the entire activity, measures the hold which the activity, as one whole affair, has upon a person. It shows how much he really cares for it. We never (if we are sensible) take, in ourselves or in somebody else, the "will for the deed" unless there is evidence that there really *was* a will, a purpose; and the sole evidence is some *striving* to realize the purpose, the putting forth of effort. If conditions forbid all effort, it is not a question of "will" at all, but simply of a sympathetic wish.

This does not mean, of course, that effort is always desirable under such conditions. On the contrary, the game may not be worth the candle; the end to be reached may not be of sufficient importance to justify the expenditure of so much energy, or of running the risks of excessive strain. Judgment comes in to decide such matters, and speaking generally it is as much a sign of bad judgment to keep on at *all* costs in an activity once entered upon, as it is a sign of weakness to be turned from it at the first evidence of difficulties. The principle laid down shows that effort is significant not as *bare* effort, or strain, but in connection with carrying forward an activity to its fulfillment: it all depends, as we say, upon the end.

Two considerations follow. (1) On the one hand, when an activity persists in spite of its temporary blocking by an obstacle, there is a situation of *mental* stress: a peculiar emotional condition of combined desire and aversion. The end continues to make an appeal, and to hold one to the activity in spite of its interruption by difficulties. This continued forward appeal gives desire. The obstacle, on the other hand, in the degree in which it arrests or thwarts progress ahead, inhibits action, and tends to divert it into some other channel — to avert action, in other words, from the original end. This gives aversion. Effort, as a mental experience, is precisely this *peculiar combination of conflicting tendencies* — tendencies away from and tendencies towards: dislike and longing.

(2) The other consideration is even more important, for it decides what happens. The emotion of effort, or of stress, is a warning to *think,*

49

to consider, to reflect, to inquire, to look into the matter. Is the end worth while under the circumstances? Is there not some other course which, under the circumstances, is better? So far as this reconsideration takes place, the situation is quite different from that of a person merely giving up as soon as an obstacle shows itself. Even if the final decision is to give up, the case is radically different from the case of giving up from mere instability of purpose. The giving up now involves an appeal to reason, and may be quite consistent with tenacity of purpose or "strength of will." However, reflection may take quite another course: it may lead not to reconsideration of ends, but to seeking for *new* means; in short, to discovery and invention also. The child who cannot carry the stone that he wishes may neither keep on in a fruitless struggle to achieve the impossible, nor yet surrender his purpose; he may be led to think of some other way of getting the stone into motion; he may try prying it along with a bar. "Necessity is the mother of invention."

In the latter case, the obstacle has, indeed,

EFFORT, THINKING, AND MOTIVATION

diverted energy; but the significant thing is that energy is *diverted into thinking;* into an intelligent consideration of the situation and of available ways and means. The really important matter in the experience of effort concerns its connection with thought. The question is not the amount of sheer strain involved, but the way in which the *thought of an end* persists in spite of difficulties, and induces a person to reflect upon the nature of the obstacles and the available resources by which they may be dealt with.

A person, child or adult, comes, in the course of an activity, up against some obstacle or difficulty. This experience of resistance has a double effect;—though in a given case one effect may predominate and obscure the other. One effect is weakening of the impetus in the forward direction; the existing line of action becomes more or less uncongenial because of the strain required to overcome difficulties. As a consequence, the tendency is to give up this line of action and to divert energy into some other channel. On the other hand, meeting an obstacle may enhance a person's perception of an end; may make him realize more clearly than ever he did before how much it means to him; and accordingly may brace him, invigorate him in his effort to achieve the end. Within certain limits, resistance only arouses energy; it acts as a stimulus. Only a spoiled child or pampered adult is dismayed or discouraged and turned aside, instead of being aroused, by lions in the path — unless the lions are very fierce and threatening. It is not too much to say that a normal person *demands* a certain amount of difficulty to surmount in order that he may have a full and vivid sense of what he is about, and hence have a lively interest in what he is doing.

Meeting obstacles makes a person project more definitely to himself the later and consummating period of his activity; it brings the end of his course of action *to consciousness*. He now *thinks* of what he is doing, instead of doing it blindly from instinct or habit. The result becomes a conscious aim, a guiding and inspiring purpose. In being an object of desire, it is also an object of endeavor.

This arousing and guiding function is exer-

EFFORT, THINKING, AND MOTIVATION

cised in two ways. Endeavor is steadied and made more persistent when its outcome is regarded as something to be achieved; and thought is stimulated to discover the best methods of dealing with the situation. The person who keeps on blindly pushing against an obstacle, trying to break through by main strength, is the one who acts unintelligently; the one who does not present to himself the nature of the end to be reached. He remains on the level of a struggling animal, who by mere quantity of brute strength tries to break down resistance and win to his goal. The true function of the conditions that call forth effort is, then, first, to make an individual more *conscious of the end and purpose of his actions;* secondly, to *turn his energy from blind, or thoughtless, struggle into reflective judgment.* These two phases of thought are interdependent. The thought of the result, the end as a conscious guiding purpose, leads to the search for means of achievement; it suggests appropriate courses of action to be tried. These means as considered and attempted supply a fuller content to the thought of the end. A boy starts somewhat

blindly to make a kite; in the course of his operations he comes across unexpected difficulties;
his kite does n't hold together, or it won't balance.
Unless his activity has a slight hold upon him,
he is thereby made aware more definitely of just
what he intends to make; he conceives the object
and end of his actions more distinctly and fully.
His end is now not just *a* kite, but some special
kind of a kite. Then he inquires what is the matter, what is the trouble, with his existing construction, and searches for remedial measures.
As he does this, his thought of the kite as a complete whole becomes more adequate; then he
sees his way more clearly what to do to make
the kite, and so on.

We are now in possession of a criterion for
estimating the place in an educative development
of difficulties and of effort. If one mean by a task
simply an undertaking involving difficulties that
have to be overcome, then children, youth, and
adults alike require tasks in order that there may
be continued development. But if one mean by a
task something that has no interest, makes no
appeal, that is wholly alien and hence uncongenial,

54

the matter is quite different. Tasks in the former sense are educative because they supply an indispensable stimulus to thinking, to reflective inquiry. Tasks in the latter sense signify nothing but sheer strain, constraint, and the need of some external motivation for keeping at them. They are *un*educative because they fail to introduce a clearer consciousness of ends and a search for proper means of realization. They are *mis*-educative, because they deaden and stupefy; they lead to that confused and dulled state of mind that always attends an action carried on without a realizing sense of what it is all about. They are also miseducative because they lead to dependence upon external ends; the child works simply because of the pressure of the taskmaster, and diverts his energies just in the degree in which this pressure is relaxed; or he works because of some alien inducement — to get some reward that has no intrinsic connection with what he is doing.

The question to be borne in mind is, then, two-fold: Is this person doing something too easy for him — something which has not a sufficient element of resistance to arouse his energies, especially his energies of thinking? Or is the work assigned so difficult that he has not the resources required in order to cope with it — so alien to his experience and his acquired habits that he does not know where or how to take hold? Between these two questions lies the teacher's task — for the teacher has a problem as well as the pupil. How shall the activities of pupils be progressively complicated by the introduction of difficulties, and yet these difficulties be of a nature to stimulate instead of dulling and merely discouraging? The judgment, the tact, the intellectual sympathy of instructors is taxed to the uttermost in answering these questions in the concrete with respect to the various subjects of study.

When an activity is too easy and simple, a person either engages in it because of the immediate pleasurable excitement it awakens, or he puts just enough of his powers upon it — their purely mechanical and physical side — to perform what is required in a perfunctory way, while he lets his mind wander to other things where there is at least enough novelty to keep his fancies going. Strange as it may seem to say it, one of the chief objections both to mechanical drill work and to the assigning of subject-matter too difficult for pupils is that the only activity to which they actually incite the pupils is in lines too *easy* for them. Only the powers already formed, the habits already fixed, are called into play; the mind — the power of thinking — is not called into action. Hence apathy in children naturally sluggish, or mind-wandering in children of a more imaginative nature. What happens when work too difficult, work beyond the limits of capacity, is insisted upon? If the teacher is professionally skilled, a pupil will not be able entirely to shirk or to escape. He must keep up the *form* of attentive study, and produce a result as evidence of having been occupied. Naturally he seeks short cuts; he does what he can do without recourse to processes of thinking that are beyond him. Any external and routine device is employed to "get the answer"— possibly surreptitious aid from others or downright cheating. Any way, he does what is already easiest for him to do; he follows the line of least resistance. The sole alternative is the use of initiative in thinking out the conditions of the problem and the way to go at it. And this alternative is within his reach only when the work to be done is of a nature to make an appeal to him, or to enlist his powers; and when the difficulties are such as to stimulate instead of depressing.

Good teaching, in other words, is teaching that appeals to established powers while it includes such *new* material as will demand their redirection for a new end, this redirection requiring thought — intelligent effort. In every case, the educational significance of effort, its value for an educative growth, resides in its connection with a stimulation of greater *thoughtfulness*, not in the greater strain it imposes. Educative effort is a sign of the transformation of a comparatively blind activity (whether impulsive or habitual) into a more consciously reflective one.

For the sake of completeness of statement, we will say (what hardly should now require

EFFORT, THINKING, AND MOTIVATION

statement on its own account) that such effort is in no sense a foe of interest. It is a part of the process of growth of activity from direct interest to indirect. In our previous section, we considered this development as meaning an increase of the complexity of an activity (that is, of the number of factors involved), and the increased importance of its outcome as a motive, in spite of contrary appeals, for devotion to intervening means. In this section, we have brought out more emphatically the fact that along with this increasing remoteness of the end (the longer period required for the consummation of an activity) goes a greater number of difficulties to be overcome, and the consequent need of effort. And our conclusion has been that the effort needed is secured when the activity in question is of such positive and abiding interest as to arouse the person to clearer recognition of purpose and to a more thoughtful consideration of means of accomplishment. The educator who associates difficulties and effort with *increased depth and scope of thinking* will never go far wrong. The one who associates it with sheer strain, sheer dead lift of energy, will never understand either how to secure the needed effort when it is needed nor the best way to utilize the energy aroused.

It remains to apply what has been said to the question of motivation. "Motive" is the name for the end or aim in respect to its hold on *action*, its power to *move*. It is one thing to speculate idly upon possible results, to keep them before the mind in a purely theoretical way. It is another thing for the results contemplated or projected to be so desired that the thought of them stirs endeavor. "Motive" is a name for the end in its active or dynamic capacity. It would be mere repetition of our previous analysis to show that this moving power expresses the extent to which the end foreseen is bound up with an activity with which the self is identified. It is enough to note that the motive force of an end and the interest that the end possesses are equivalent expressions of the vitality and depth of a proposed course of activity.

A word of warning may be in place against taking the idea of motivation in too *personal* a sense, in a sense too detached, that is, from the object or end in view. In the theory of instruction, as distinct from its practice, the need of motivation was for a long time overlooked or even denied. It was assumed that sheer force of will, arbitrary effort, was alone required. In practice this meant (as we have seen) appeal to extraneous sources of motivation: to reverence for the authority of teacher or text; to fear of punishment or the displeasure of others; to regard for success in adult life; to winning a prize; to standing higher than one's fellows; to fear of not being promoted, etc. The next step was taken when some educators recognized the ineffective hold of such motives upon many pupils — their lack of adequate motivating force in the concrete. They looked for motives which would have more weight with the average pupil. But too often they still conceived the motive as outside the subject-matter, something existing purely in the feelings, and giving a reason for attention to a matter that in itself would not provide a motive. They looked *for* a motive for the study or the lesson, instead of a motive *in* it. Some reason must be found in the *person*, apart from the arithmetic or the geography or the manual activity, that might be attached to the lesson material so as to give it a leverage, or moving force.

One effect was to substitute a discussion of "motives" in the abstract for a consideration of subject-matter in the concrete. The tendency was to make out a list of motives or "interests" by which children in general or children of a given age are supposed to be actuated, and then to consider how these might be linked up with the various lessons so as to impart efficacy to the latter. The important question, however, is what specific subject-matter is so connected with the growth of the child's existing concrete capabilities as to give it a moving force. What is needed is not an inventory of personal motives which we suppose children to have, but a consideration of their *powers*, their tendencies in action, and the ways in which these can be carried forward by a given subject-matter.

If a child has, for example, an artistic capacity in the direction of music or drawing, it is not necessary to find a motive for its exercise. The problem is not to find a motive, but to find material of and conditions for its exercise. Any material that appeals to this capacity has by that very fact motivating force. The end or object in its vital connection with the person's activities *is* a motive.

Another consequence of a too personal conception of motivation is a narrow and external conception of use and function. It is justifiable to ask for the utility of any educational subject-matter. But use may be estimated from different standpoints. We may have a readymade conception of use or function, and try the value of what is learned by its conformity to this standard. In this case we shall not regard any pursuit as properly motivated, unless we see that it performs some special office that we have laid down as useful or practical. But if we start from the standpoint of the active powers of the children concerned, we shall measure the utility of new subject-matter and new modes of skill by the way in which they promote the growth of these powers. We shall not insist upon tangible material products, nor upon what is learned being

put to further use at once in some visible way.
nor even demand evidence that the children
have become morally improved in some respect :
save as the growth of powers is itself a moral
gain.

IV

TYPES OF EDUCATIVE INTEREST

THE clew we have followed in our discussion of interest is its connection with an activity engaging a person in a whole-hearted way. Interest is not some one thing; it is a name for the fact that a course of action, an occupation, or pursuit absorbs the powers of an individual in a thorough-going way. But an activity cannot go on in a void. It requires material, subject-matter, conditions upon which to operate. On the other hand, it requires certain tendencies, habits, powers on the part of the self. Wherever there is genuine interest, there is an identification of these two things. The person acting finds his own well-being bound up with the development of an object to its own issue. If the activity goes a certain way, then a subject-matter is carried to a certain result, and a person achieves a certain satisfaction.

There is nothing new or striking in the conception of activity as an important educational principle. In the form of the idea of " self-activity " in particular, it has long been a name for the ultimate educational ideal. But activity has often been interpreted in too formal and too internal a sense, and hence has remained a barren ideal without influence on practice; sometimes it becomes a mere phrase, receiving the homage of the lips only. To make the idea of activity effective, we must take it broadly enough to cover all the doings that involve growth of power — especially of power to realize the *meaning* of what is done. This excludes action done under external constraint or dictation, for this has no significance for the mind of him who performs it. It excludes also mere random reaction to an excitation that is finished when the momentary act has ceased — which does not, in other words, carry the person acting into future broader fields. It also excludes action so habitual that it has become routine or mechanical. Unfortunately action from external constraint, for mere love of excitement and from mechanical force of habit are so common that these exceptions cover much ground. But the ground lying within these excepted fields is the ground where an educative process is *not* going on.

The kinds of activity remaining as true educative interests vary indefinitely with age, with individual native endowments, with prior experience, with social opportunities. It is out of the question to try to catalogue them. But we may discriminate some of their more general aspects, and thereby, perhaps, make the connection of interest with educational practice somewhat more concretely obvious. Since one of the main reasons for taking self-activity in a formal sense was ignoring the importance of the body and of bodily instinct, we may well begin with interest in activity in this most direct and literal sense.

1. It is an old story that the human young have to *learn* most of the things that the young of other animals do instinctively or else with a slight amount of trying. Reflection on this fact shows that in learning these things human offspring are brought to the need of learning other things, and also to acquiring a habit of learning —a love of learning. While these considerations are fairly familiar, we often overlook their bear-

ing upon the fact of physical activities. It follows from them at once that in so far as a physical activity has to be *learned*, it is not merely physical, but is mental, intellectual, in quality. The first problem set the human young is learning to use the organs of sense — the eye, ear, touch, etc. — and of movement — the muscles — in connection with one another. Of course, some of the mastery achieved does not involve much mental experimentation, but is due to the ripening of physiological connections. But nevertheless there is a genuinely intellectual factor when the child learns that one kind of eye-activity means a certain kind of moving of the arm, clasping of the fingers, etc., and that this in turn entails a certain kind of exploring with the fingers, resulting in experience of smoothness, etc. In such cases, there is not simply an acquisition of a new physical capacity; there is also learning in the mental sense; something has been found out. The rapidity of mental development in the first year and a half of infancy, the whole-hearted intentness and absorption of the growing baby in his activities, the joy that accompanies his increase of ability to

control his movements — all of these things are
object-lessons, writ large, as to the nature of interest, and the intellectual significance of actions
that (externally judged) are physical.

This period of growth occurs, of course, before
children go to school ; at least before they go to
anything called school. But the amount and the
mode of learning in this school of action is most
significant in revealing the importance of types
of occupation within the school involving the
exercise of senses and movement. One of the
reasons (as already indicated) for the slight advance made in putting in practice the doctrine of
self-activity (with its recommendation of mental
initiative and intellectual self-reliance, and its
attacks upon the idea of pouring in and passive
absorption) is precisely that it was supposed that
self-activity could be secured purely internally,
without the coöperation of bodily action through
play, construction of objects, and manipulation
of materials and tools. Only with children having specialized intellectual abilities is it possible
to secure mental activity without participation
of the organs of sense and the muscles. Yet how

much of elementary schooling has consisted in the imposition of forms of discipline intended to *repress* all activity of the body! Under such a régime it is not surprising that children are found to be naturally averse to learning, or that intellectual activity is found to be so foreign to their nature that they have to be coerced or cunningly coaxed to engage in it! So educators blamed the children or the perverseness of human nature, instead of attacking the conditions which, by divorcing learning from use of the natural organs of action, made learning both difficult and onerous.

The teachings of Pestalozzi and of the sense-training and object-lesson schools in pedagogy were the first important influence in challenging the supremacy of a purely formal, because inner and abstract, conception of self-activity. But, unfortunately, the psychology of the times was still associated with a false physiology and a false philosophy of the relations of mind and body. The senses were supposed to be the inlets, the avenues, the gateways, of knowledge, or at least of the raw materials of knowledge. It was not known that the sense-organs are simply the pathways of *stimuli to motor-responses*, and that it is only through these motor-responses, and especially through consideration of the adapting of sense-stimulus and motor-response to each other that growth of knowledge occurs. The sense-qualities of color, sound, contact, etc., are important not in their mere reception and storage, but in their connection with the various forms of behavior that secure intelligent control. The baby would not arrive even at the knowledge of individual things, — hat, chair, orange, stone, tree, — were it not for the active responses through which various qualities are made mutually significant of one another, and thereby knit into coherent wholes. Even in the ordinary hard-and-fast school, where it is thought to be a main duty to suppress all forms of motor-activity, the physical activities that are still allowed under the circumstances, such as moving the eyes, lips, etc., in reading to one's self; the physical adjustments of reading aloud, figuring, writing, reciting, are much more important than is generally recognized in holding attention. The outlet in action is so scanty and so accidental, however, that much energy remains unutilized and hence ready to break forth in mischief or worse ; while mind takes flights of uncontrolled fancy, day-dreaming and wandering to all sorts of subjects.

The next great advance in the development of a more real, less arbitrary conception of activity, came with Froebel and the kindergarten movement. Plays, games, occupations of a consecutive sort, requiring both construction and manipulation, were recognized, practically for the first time since Plato, as of essential educational importance. The place of the exercise of bodily functions in the growth of mind was practically acknowledged. But the use of the principle was still hampered and distorted by a false physiology and psychology. The *direct* contribution to growth made by the free and full control of bodily organs, of physical materials and appliances in the realization of purposes, was not understood. Hence the value of the physical side of play, games, occupations, the use of gifts, etc., was explained by recourse to *indirect* consideration — by symbolism. It was supposed that the educative development was not on account of what was directly done, but because of certain ultimate philosophical and spiritual principles which the activities somehow symbolically stood for. Save for the danger of introducing an element of unreality and so of sentimentality, this misinterpretation of the source of value in the kindergarten activities would not have been so serious had it not reacted very decisively upon the selection and organization of materials and activities. The disciples of Froebel were not free to take plays and modes of occupation upon their own merits; they had to select and arrange them in accordance with certain alleged principles of symbolism, as related to a supposed law of the unfolding of an enfolded Absolute Whole. Certain raw materials and lines of action shown by experience outside the school to be of great value were excluded because the principles of symbolic interpretation did not apply to them. These same principles led, moreover, to an exaggerated preference for geometrically abstract forms, and to insistence upon rigid adherence to a highly elaborate technique for dealing with

73

them. Only within the last generation have the advances of science and philosophy brought about recognition of the direct value of actions and a freer utilization of play and occupational activities. Conceived in this freer and more scientific way, the principles of Froebel undoubtedly represent the greatest advance yet made in the recognition of the possibilities of bodily action in educative growth. The methods of Montessori are based on a like recognition, with the advantage of additional technical knowledge; and if the tendency to reduce them to isolated mechanical exercises (a tendency unfortunately attendant upon the spread of every definitely formulated system) can be resisted or overcome, they undoubtedly suggest further resources that can be utilized with younger children, or with older children whose sensori-motor development has been retarded.

2. In this discussion of physical activity I have had in mind for the most part that of the organs of the body, especially the hands, as employed directly with simple materials, or at most such simple appliances as a pencil, a brush, etc.

74

TYPES OF EDUCATIVE INTEREST

A higher form of activity involving the sensori-motor apparatus of the body is found when the control over external objects is achieved by means of tools of some sort, or by the application of one material to another. The use of a saw, a gimlet, a plane, of modeling-sticks, etc., illustrate the intervention of tools. The use of a thread in sewing, the application of heat and moisture in cooking or other simple experimentations, illustrate the use of one thing (or mode of energy) to bring about a change in another thing. There is, of course, no sharp distinction, either in practice or in principle, between this form of activity and the more direct kind just discussed. The organs of the body — especially the hands — may be regarded as a kind of tools whose use is to be learned by trying and thinking. Tools may be regarded as a sort of extension of the bodily organs. But the growing use of the latter opens a new line of development so important in its consequences that it is worth while to give it distinctive recognition. It is the *discovery and use of extra-organic tools which has made possible, both in the history of the race and of the individual, complicated activities of a long dur-ation*—that is, with results that are long post-poned. And, as we have already seen, it is this prolongation and postponement which requires an increasing use of intelligence. The use of tools and appliances (in the broad sense) also demands a greater degree of technical skill than does mastery of the use of the natural organs — or rather, it involves the problem of a progressively more complicated use of the latter — and hence stimulates a new line of development.

Roughly speaking, the use of such intervening appliances marks off games and work on one side, from play on the other. For a time children are satisfied with such changes as they can bring about with their hands and by locomotion and transportation. Other changes which they cannot so effect they are satisfied to *imagine*, without an actual physical modification. Let us "play" — let us "make-believe" that things are so and so, suffices. One thing may be made to stand for another, irrespective of its actual fitness. Thus leaves become dishes, bright stones articles of food, splinters of wood knives and forks, when children are playing at setting a table. In free play things are plastic to alter their nature as mood or passing need dictates; chairs now serve as wagons, now as a train of cars, now as boats, etc. In games, however, there are rules to be followed; so that things have to be used in *definite* ways, since they are means for accomplishing definite ends, as a club is a bat for hitting a ball. In similar fashion, children as their powers mature want real dishes, real articles of food; and are better satisfied if they can actually make a fire and cook. They want to use the things that are fitted to their purposes and that will really accomplish certain results, instead of effecting them only in fancy. It will be found that the change comes with ability to carry a purpose in mind for a longer time. The little child is impatient, as we say, for immediate returns. He cannot wait to get the appropriate means and use them in the appropriate way to achieve the end: not because he is physically more impatient than older persons, but because an end that is not achieved almost at once gets away from his mind. To execute his purpose he makes his "means" realize his ideas at one stroke of the magic wand of imagination. But as ideas persist for a longer time they can be employed to effect an actual transformation of conditions — a process that almost always requires the intervention of tools, or the use of intervening appliances.

There seems to be no better name for the acts of using *intermediate* means, or appliances, to reach ends than *work*. When employed in this way, however, work must be distinguished from labor and from toil and drudgery. Labor means a form of work in which the direct result accomplished is of value only as a means of exchange for something else. It is an *economic* term, being applied to that form of work where the product is paid for, and the money paid is used for objects of more direct values. Toil implies unusual arduousness in a task, involving fatigue. Drudgery is an activity which in itself is quite disagreeable, performed under the constraint of some quite extraneous need. Play and work cannot, therefore, be distinguished from one another according to the presence or absence of direct interest in what is doing. A child engaged in making something with tools, say, a boat, may be just as immediately interested in what he is doing as if he were sailing the boat. He is not doing what he does for the mere sake of an external result — the boat — nor for the mere sake of sailing it later. The thought of the finished product and of the use to which it is to be put may come to his mind, but so as to enhance his immediate activity of construction. In this case, his interest is free. He has a play-motive; his activity is essentially artistic in principle. What differentiates it from more spontaneous play is an *intellectual* quality; a remoter end in time serves to suggest and regulate a series of acts. Not to introduce an element of work *in this sense* when the child is ready for it is simply arbitrarily to arrest his development, and to force his activities to a level of sense-excitation after he is prepared to act upon the basis of an idea. A mode of activity that was quite normal in its own period becomes disintegrating when persisted in after a person is ripe for an activity involving more thought. We must also remember that the change from an activity with an end near by to one with an end farther off does not come all at once, nor at the same time with respect to all things. A child may be ready for occupation with tools like scissors, paint and brush, for setting a table, cooking, etc., while with respect to other activities he is still unable to plan and arrange ahead. Thus there is no ground for the assumption that children of kindergarten age are capable only of make-believe play, while children of the primary grades should be held to all work and no play. Only the false idea about symbolism leads to the former conclusion; and only a false identification of interest and play with trivial amusement leads to the latter conclusion. It has been said that man is man only as he plays; to say this involves some change from the meaning in which play has just been used. But in the broader sense of whole-hearted identification with what one is doing —in the sense of completeness of interest, it is so true that it should be a truism.

Work in the sense in which it has been defined covers all activities involving the use of

80

intervening materials, appliances, and forms of skill consciously used in achieving results. It covers all forms of expression and construction with tools and materials, all forms of artistic and manual activity so far as they involve the conscious or thoughtful endeavor to achieve an end. They include, that is, painting, drawing, clay modeling, singing so far as there is any conscious attention to means — to the technique of execution. They comprehend the various forms of manual training, work with wood, metal, textiles, cooking, sewing, etc., so far as these involve an idea of the result to be accomplished (instead of working from dictation or an external model which does away with the need for thought). They cover also the manual side of scientific inquiry, the collection of materials for study, the management of apparatus, the sequence of acts required in carrying on and in recording experiments.

3. So far as this latter interest — the interest in discovery or in finding out what happens under given circumstances — gains in importance, there develops a third type of interest — the distinc-

tively intellectual interest. Our wording should be carefully noted. The intellectual interest is not a new thing, now showing itself for the first time. Our discussion of the development of the so-called physical activities of a baby, and of the constructive work of children, youth, and adults has been intended to show that intelligence, in the form of clear perception of the result of an activity and search for and adaptation of means, should be an integral part of such activities. But it is possible for this intellectual interest to be subordinate, to be subsidiary, to the accomplishment of a process. But it is also possible for it to become a dominating interest, so that instead of thinking things out and discovering them for the sake of the successful achievement of an activity, we institute the activity for the sake of finding out something. Then the distinctively intellectual, or theoretical, interest shows itself.

As there is no sharp line of division in theory, so there is none in practice. Planning ahead, taking notice of what happens, relating this to what is attempted, are parts of all intelligent or purposive activities. It is the business of educators to see that the conditions of expression of the practical interests are such as to encourage the developing of these intellectual phases of an activity, and thereby evoke a gradual transition to the theoretical type. It is a commonplace that the fundamental principle of science is connected with the relation of cause and effect. Interest in this relation begins on the practical side. Some effect is aimed at, is desired and worked for, and attention is given to the conditions for producing it. At first the interest in the achievement of the end predominates; but in the degree in which this interest is bound up with *thoughtful* effort, interest in the end or effect is of necessity transferred to the interest in the means — the causes — which bring it about. Where work with tools, gardening, cooking, etc., is intelligently carried on, it is comparatively a simple matter to secure a transfer of interest from the practical side to experimentation for the sake of discovery. When any one becomes interested in a problem as a problem and in inquiry and learning for the sake of solving the problem, interest is distinctively intellectual.

4. Social interest, interest in persons, is a strong special interest, and also one which intertwines with those already named. Small children's concern with persons is remarkably intense. Their dependence upon others for support and guidance, if nothing else, provides a natural basis for attention to people and for a wish to enter into intimate connections with them. Then distinctively social instincts, such as sympathy, imitation, love of approval, etc., come in. Children's contact with other persons is continuous; and there are practically no activities of a child that are isolated. His own activities are so bound up with others, and what others do touches him so deeply and in so many ways, that it is only at rare moments, perhaps of a clash of wills, that a child draws a sharp line between other peoples' affairs as definitely theirs and his own as exclusively his. His father and mother, his brothers and sisters, his home, his friends are *his;* they belong to his idea of himself. If they were cut away from his thought of himself, and from his

hopes, desires, plans, and experiences, the latter would lose pretty much all their contents. Because of limitations of experience and of intelligence, there are many affairs of others that a child cannot make his own; but within these limits a child's identification of his own concerns with those of others is naturally even more intense than that of grown persons. He has not come into business rivalries with them; the number of people whom he meets who are not sympathetic with his concerns is small; it is through entering into the actions of others, directly and imaginatively, that he finds the most significant and the most rewarding of all his experiences. In these regards, a child is likely to be more social in his interests than the average adult.

This social interest not only, then, interfuses and permeates his interest in his own actions and sufferings, but it also suffuses his interest in *things*. Adults are so accustomed to making a sharp distinction between their relations to things and to other persons; their pursuits in life are so largely specialized along the line of having to do with things just as things, that it is difficult for them, practically impossible, to realize the extent to which children are concerned with things only as they enter into and affect the concerns of persons, and the extent to which a personal-social interest radiates upon objects and gives them their meaning and worth. A moment's consideration of children's plays shows how largely they are sympathetic and dramatic reproductions of social activities; and thereby affords a clew to the extent in which interest in things is borrowed from their ideas of what people do to and with things. Much of the so-called animistic tendency of children, their tendency to personify natural objects and events, is at bottom nothing but an overflow of their social interests. It is not so much that they literally conceive things to be alive, as that things are of interest to them only when they are encompassed with the interests they see exemplified in persons; otherwise things are, at first, more or less matters of indifference to them.

No doubt some of the repulsiveness of purely abstract intellectual studies to many children is simply the reflex of the fact that the things — the

86

facts and truths — presented to them have been isolated from their human context. This does not mean, of course, that a mythological or fanciful human character should be attributed to inanimate things; but it does mean that impersonal material should be presented so far as possible in the rôle it actually plays in life. Children generally begin the study of geography, for example, with a social interest so strong that it is fairly romantic. Their imaginations are fired by the thought of learning how strange and far-away peoples live and fare. Then they are fed on abstract definitions and classifications; or, what is almost as deadening, upon bare physical facts about the forms of land and water, the structure of continents, etc. Then there are complaints that children have so little interest in the study — simply because they have not been touched where they are at home. In such sciences as physics and chemistry there are enough facts and principles which are associated with human concerns to supply adequate material for thorough grounding in the methods of those sciences.

It is not necessary to do more than to allude

to the close connection between social and moral interests.[1] In those cases where direct interest points one way and obligation another, no reinforcement of the demand of duty is as strong as that furnished by a realization of the interests of others that are bound up with it. The abstract idea of duty, like other abstract ideas, has naturally little motivating force. Social interests have a powerful hold, which, by association, is transferred to what is morally required. Thus a strong indirect interest resists the contrary pull of immediate inclination. The only other moral point that need be mentioned here is that the conception of interest as naturally a selfish or egoistic principle is wholly irreconcilable with the facts of the case. All interest is naturally in *objects* that carry an activity forward or in *objects* that mark its fulfillment; hence the character of the interest depends upon the nature of these objects. If they are low, or unworthy, or purely selfish, then so is the interest, but not otherwise. The strength of the interest in other persons and in their activities and aims is a

[1] See *Moral Principles in Education*, in this *Series.*

88

natural resource for making activities broad, generous, and enlightened in scope; while the physical, manual, and scientific interests in their identification with *objects* make for a broadening of the self.

V

THE PLACE OF INTEREST IN THE THEORY OF EDUCATION

WE conclude with a brief restatement setting forth the importance of the idea of interest for educational theory. Interests, as we have noted, are very varied; every impulse and habit that generates a purpose having sufficient force to move a person to strive for its realization, becomes an interest. But in spite of this diversity, interests are one in principle. They all mark an identification in action, and hence in desire, effort, and thought, of self with objects; with, namely, the objects in which the activity terminates (ends) and with the objects by which it is carried forward to its end (means). Interest, in the emotional sense of the word, is the evidence of the way in which the self is engaged, occupied, taken up with, concerned in, absorbed by, carried away by, this objective subject-matter. At bottom all misconceptions of interest, whether in practice

or in theory, come from ignoring or excluding its
moving, developing nature; they bring an activity
to a standstill, cut up its progressive growth into
a series of static cross-sections. When this happens, nothing remains but to identify interest
with the momentary excitation an object arouses.
Such a relation of object and self is not only
not educative, but it is worse than nothing. It
dissipates energy, and forms a habit of dependence upon such meaningless excitations, a habit
most adverse to sustained thought and endeavor.
Wherever such practices are resorted to in the
name of interest, they very properly bring it into
disrepute. It is not enough to *catch* attention;
it must be *held*. It does not suffice to arouse
energy; the *course* that energy takes, the results
that it effects are the important matters.

But since activities, even those originally impulsive, are more or less continuous or enduring,
such static, non-developing excitements, represent not interest, but an abnormal set of conditions. The positive contributions of the idea of
interest to pedagogic theory are twofold. In
the first place, it protects us from a merely

internal conception of mind; and, in the second place, from a merely *external* conception of subject-matter.

(1) Any one who has grasped the conception of an interest as an activity that moves toward an end, developing as it proceeds thought of this end and search for means, will never fall into the error of thinking of mind (or of the self) as an isolated inner world by itself. It will be apparent that mind is one with intelligent or purposeful activity — with an activity that *means* something and in which the meaning counts as a factor in the development of an activity. There is a sense in which mind is measured by growth of power of abstraction, and a very important sense this is. There is another sense in which it can be truly said that abstractness is the worst evil that infests education. The false sense of abstraction is connected with thinking of mental activity as something that can go on wholly by itself, apart from objects or from the world of persons and things. Real subject-matter being removed, something else has to be supplied in its place for the mind to occupy itself with. This

something else must of necessity be mere sym-
bols; that is to say things that are not signs *of*
anything, because the first-hand subject-matter
which gives them meaning has been excluded
or at least neglected. Or when objects — concrete facts, etc. — are introduced, it is as mere
occasions for the mind to exercise its own separate powers — just as dumb-bells or pulleys and
weights are a mere occasion for exercising the
muscles. The world of studies then becomes a
strange and peculiar world, because a world cut
off from — abstracted from — the world in which
pupils as human beings live and act and suffer.
Lack of "interest," lack of power to hold attention and stir thought, are a necessary consequence of the unreality attendant upon such a
realm for study. Then it is concluded that the
"minds" of children or of people in general are
averse to learning, are indifferent to the concerns of intelligence. But such indifference and
aversion are always evidence — either directly
or as a consequence of previous bad conditions
— that the appropriate conditions for the exercise of mind are not there : — that they are ex-

cluded because there has been no provision of situations in which things have to be intelligently dealt with. Everything that is disparaging in the common use of the terms academic, abstract, formal, theoretical, has its roots here.[1]

(2) The supposed externality of subject-matter is but the counterpart phase of the alleged internal isolation of mind. If mind means certain powers or faculties existing in themselves and needing only to be exercised *by* and *upon* presented subject-matter, the presented subject-matter must mean something complete in its ready-made and fixed separateness. Objects, facts, truths of geography, history, and science not being conceived as means and ends for the intelligent development of experience, are thought of just as stuff to be learned. Reading, writing, figuring are mere external forms of skill to be mastered. Even the arts — drawing, singing — are thought of as meaning so many ready-made things, pictures, songs, that are to be externally produced

[1] Of course, nothing that is said here is meant to depreciate the wonderful possibilities involved in an *imaginative experimentation* with things, *after* the conditions of more direct transactions with them have been met.

and reproduced. Then we have the situation described in the early portion of this essay: Some means must be found to overcome the separation of mind and subject-matter; problems of method in teaching are reduced to various ways of overcoming a gap which exists only because a radically *wrong method* had already been entered upon. The doctrine of interest is not a short cut to "methods" of this sort. On the contrary, it is a warning to furnish conditions such that the natural impulses and acquired habits, as far as they are desirable, *shall obtain subject-matter and modes of skill* in order to develop to their natural ends of achievement and efficiency. Interest, the identification of mind with the material and methods of a developing activity, is the inevitable result of the presence of such situations.

Hence it follows that little can be accomplished by setting up "interest" as an end or a method by itself. Interest is obtained not by thinking about it and consciously aiming at it, *but by considering and aiming at the conditions* that lie back of it, and compel it. If we can discover a child's urgent needs and powers, and if we can supply an environment of materials, appliances, and resources — physical, social, and intellectual — to direct their adequate operation, we shall not have to think about interest. It will take care of itself. For mind will have met with what it needs in order to *be* mind. The problem of educators, teachers, parents, the state, is to provide the environment that induces educative or developing activities, and where these are found the one thing needful in education is secured.

OUTLINE

I. UNIFIED VERSUS DIVIDED ACTIVITY.

II. INTEREST AS DIRECT AND INDIRECT

OUTLINE

OUTLINE

99

OUTLINE

OUTLINE

TEXTUAL NOTE: The text of *Interest and Effort in Education* published here is a photo-offset reprint of the first printing (Boston: Houghton Mifflin Company, The Riverside Press, 1913). No emendations have been made in the text. The Preface by James E. Wheeler substitutes for the Editor's Introduction by Henry Suzzallo.

J. A. B.